1993
WORLD YOUTH DAY
DENVER, COLORADO USA

ELLEN JASKOL

"Jesus has called each one of you to Denver for a purpose. You must live these days in such a way that, when the time comes to return home, each one of you will have a clearer idea of what Christ expects of you."

— Pope John Paul II

ROCKY MOUNTAIN NEWS

THE NORTH AMERICAN JOURNEY OF HIS HOLINESS
THE POPE
JOHN PAUL II

ANDREWS AND McMEEL

A Universal Press Syndicate Company

Kansas City

Edited and Designed By
J. BRUCE BAUMANN

Text By
CHRISTOPHER CUBBISON

Director of Photography
JANET REEVES

Staff Photographers
**GLENN ASAKAWA
STEVE GROER
ELLEN JASKOL
THOMAS KELSEY
GEORGE KOCHANIEC JR.
JAY KOELZER
DEAN KRAKEL
LINDA McCONNELL
CYRUS McCRIMMON
FRANK MURRAY
KEN PAPALEO
DENNIS SCHROEDER
HAL STOELZLE**

Staff Picture Editors
**DAVID DENNEY
RICK GIASE
VERN WALKER**

Lab Technician
LISA GRIFFIN

Technical Advisor
BILL KYLE

Copy Editor
MARK CHRISTOPHER

ROCKY MOUNTAIN NEWS

LARRY D. STRUTTON
PUBLISHER, PRESIDENT & CEO

JAY AMBROSE
EDITOR

ACKNOWLEDGMENTS

This book would not have been possible without the contributions of the entire newsroom staff of the Rocky Mountain News. Special thanks to religion writer Gary Massaro, who began covering the pope's pilgrimage to Denver in early 1992 and who traveled to Rome four times, along with photographer Ellen Jaskol, to cover these events.

COVER PHOTOGRAPH: A study in spiritual intensity, Pope John Paul II prays during a Mass for his bishops at the Cathedral of the Immaculate Conception in Denver. *Photographed by Hal Stoelzle*

ISBN: 0-8362-8042-3

Library of Congress Catalog Card Number: 93-73047

Pope John Paul II greets 250,000 pilgrims at the prayer vigil at Cherry Creek State Park.

The Holy Father prays during his meeting with Colorado Catholics at McNichols Arena. A giant television screen captures his image for the 18,000 in attendance.

I came so that they might have life, and have it more abundantly. (John 10:10)

—Theme for World Youth Day 1993

A PILGRIMAGE TO DENVER

THEY came from remote, dust-blown villages in southern Colorado, alpine hamlets in Switzerland, the teeming urban centers of Paris, Chicago and Buenos Aires.

They hailed from Mexico and Malaysia, Haiti and Honduras, Australia and Austria, Belgium and Bosnia-Herzegovina, Nigeria and Nicaragua, and from across the United States and Canada.

Some prosperous, some destitute, they came from more than 100 countries on a mission to shape their spiritual future. They were drawn by their faith, a thirst for adventure and reverence for a man who inspired them toward goodness.

For five days at the foot of Colorado's majestic Rocky Mountains, 186,000 young apostles of Christianity infused a city, a church and themselves with righteous zeal.

They were the largest single gathering of people in the history of the Rocky Mountain West.

When Pope John Paul II landed at Stapleton International Airport on August 12, 1993, as a midafternoon downpour erupted, Bill Clinton, the young American president, greeted him warmly.

Rome — and, in a very real sense, the whole world — had come to Denver.

For the young people of World Youth Day, it was part tent revival, part summer camp, part holy sacrament, part blunt reckoning with their future.

For His Holiness, Pope John Paul II, it was a precious opportunity to touch the generation that will carry the largest Christian religion into the next millennium.

For Denver and all of Colorado, well, it was a spectacle to behold.

• • • •

I have chosen the city of Denver.

With those seven words in St. Peter's Square on Palm Sunday 1992, Pope John Paul II set in motion the events that would converge 16 months later in the American heartland.

The first non-Italian pope in 450 years, Karol Wojtyla of Wadowice, Poland, had made international travel a hallmark of his papacy. The journey to Jamaica, Mexico and Denver was his 60th foreign trip since being elected pope October 16, 1978. It was his third trip to the United States but the first in six years.

Another trademark of this first Polish pope was his delight in young people. Their energy and idealism seemed to electrify him.

At 73, John Paul II was not as healthy and vigorous as he once had been. He had survived an assassin's bullet and major abdominal surgery. He often walked hunch-shouldered, leaning on a staff. But when he approached children, a change came over him. He stood straighter. A smile spread warmly across his face.

The pope knew that young people were the church's future. To dramatize his commitment to them, he had initiated World Youth Day in the Vatican on Palm Sunday, 1984. Since 1987, it has been held outside Italy in odd-numbered years. First came Buenos Aires, Argentina, then Santiago de Compostela, Spain. In August 1991, the scene was Czestochowa in the pope's native Poland, in the heart of the fast-crumbling Soviet Communist empire.

The United States, the pope decided, would be the site of World Youth Day 1993. Dioceses the pope had never visited were asked to submit proposals. Minneapolis-St. Paul, Buffalo, N.Y., and Chicago responded. So did Denver.

John Paul was drawn to Denver for more than one reason. The Vatican saw Denver as a modern city that would be an attractive venue for the pope to re-emphasize longstanding church teachings with the next generation of Catholics. World Youth Day, the pope wrote, would "provide an opportunity for many young people to make bold and enlightened choices which can help steer the future course of history under the powerful but gentle guidance of the Holy Spirit."

The mountains and temperate climate were another big draw. His two previous trips to the United States had taken him to big cities on both coasts and centers of Catholicism in the interior, but he'd never seen America's mountains. The pope was an avid sportsman in his younger days, and his love for solitary walks in Italy's northern mountains had been well-documented.

When Denver journalists visiting the Vatican in March 1993 gave the pope a framed color photograph of the city's skyline, set against the Rockies, he beamed and said, "Ah, mountains. A modern city."

For Denver, the pope's pilgrimage would further gild the city's coming of age. Moving toward the new century on a resurgent economy and boasting the world's newest mega-airport, a strikingly modern skyline and a wildly popular new major league baseball team, Denver was on a roll.

A public extravaganza featuring the world's most influential religious leader, the president of the United States, 186,000 enthusiastic faithful and 3,000 accredited journalists from around the world — it was hard to imagine a prouder moment in the city's 134-year history.

• • • •

THE pope's selection of Denver as World Youth Day's host city was one thing. Getting Denver ready for it was quite another.

The Mile High City had never hosted anything so massive. The 1859 Gold Rush days of Denver's infancy brought about 50,000 settlers and prospectors. But they didn't all arrive in one week.

In contemporary times, colossal events skipped Colorado. Super Bowls went to warm-weather cities. Colorado voters nixed the state's bid to land the 1976 Winter Olympics.

Denver had bulged in 1988 when the International Lions Club convention brought 35,000 delegates to town. Now, the city would accommodate 186,000 guests for almost a week. On the final day, about 375,000 people would fill Cherry Creek State Park to witness the papal Mass.

In the frantic final days before the pope's arrival, an army of technicians and laborers descended on the centers of activity of World Youth Day — the state park, downtown's Civic Center Park (renamed Celebration Plaza for the week), McNichols Arena and Mile High Stadium. They installed lights, altars, camera platforms, food and merchandise tents, thousands of miles of wiring, signs in multiple languages.

In a suite of offices on the 15th floor of a downtown glass tower, World Youth Day's logistical nerve center whirred with activity. For staff members and volunteers, the sternest challenge was finding places for tens of thousands of delegates to sleep.

Front Range hotels housed almost 30,000. Workers set up 7,500 cots at the National Western Stock Show Arena on the northern fringes of the city. Another 4,000 went up in a cavernous downtown parking garage. Public buildings, school gymnasiums and Denver's Catholic parishes lodged thousands more. Several Protestant churches, in an ecumenical gesture, opened their doors. Thirteen thousand families in metropolitan Denver took in young believers.

Once housed, the young people would have to be picked up every morning, driven to the day's events and dropped off every night. The task for World Youth Day was to create a new bus system — for one week.

The mood at headquarters — soft-spoken but unrelentingly determined — mirrored the style of the man for whom World Youth Day was a lifetime's triumph.

J. Francis Stafford, 61, had been the Denver archbishop since 1986. The spiritual leader of 330,000 Catholics in central and northern Colorado, the rosy-cheeked Stafford had been pivotal in convincing the Vatican to select Denver for World Youth Day.

The Vatican's decision made it clear the pope held Stafford in high esteem. Stafford had been unfailingly loyal to the pope and key church doctrines — opposition to abortion, birth control and women in the clergy, to name just three — that many Catholics in the archbishop's own realm questioned.

• • • •

AS WAVES of World Youth Day young people reached Denver, they quickly made their presence known. They were innocent, sometimes naive, uniformly joyous.

They were full of Jesus. They used hand signals to overcome vast language barriers. They sang. They exchanged animated greetings.

A bedazzled Denver was swept off its feet. Street-hardened police officers gaped in amazement. They'd never encountered such well-behaved crowds.

"When I hold up my hand, they stop," marveled one traffic cop helping guide endless columns of kids across one of the city's busiest streets.

Most of the young people had no way to get to the imposing mountains a few miles away. But many were far more interested anyway in part of Americana much closer at hand — the Sixteenth Street Mall.

A mile-long corridor of shops and restaurants stitched together by lumbering, free buses, the mall fascinated the visitors.

They gawked. They jabbered. They absorbed.

But many of them bought nothing. Young people from Ghana, Bolivia, Thailand and other impoverished countries had not come to Denver for a shopping spree. Some of them were lucky to have scraped together $100 to carry them through a 10-day stay. Their meals and lodging generally were arranged in advance, but discretionary income was scant. For many, the only purchase would be a small gift for their family.

Denver swelled mightily with the tide of Catholics, arriving by the thousands at the airport, train station and bus depot and in cramped vehicles on the highways. There was some confusion at first about where everyone should go — to register, get meal tickets, find the right bus. But good-naturedness abounded.

At McNichols Arena, weary delegates waited in the baking sun to register. Jettisoning knapsacks, they sat down to rest with the friends they had accompanied from home. The small groups kept mostly to themselves.

And then something extraordinary began to happen. Energy began to flow.

"I'm just going to introduce myself to anyone and everyone," announced Dorothy Mack of Springfield, Mass., starting to work the crowd.

The pope greets an International Youth Forum delegate after his Mass for them Saturday. The pope likened the 270 delegates to the 12 apostles of Jesus who spread his teachings to mankind.

On the hot asphalt ringing the arena, language and cultural differences melted away. Guitars were unsheathed. Songs floated into the breeze. Arms wrapped around the shoulders of new friends. And then the McNichols parking lot filled with one giant, joyous conga line.

These young people had a very special brand of exuberance to share with the city. It was contagious.

"It's cool to be Catholic," crowed a hand-lettered banner carried by a girl getting off the train from New York at Union Station.

Once settled in for the week, this young vanguard of nearly 1 billion Roman Catholics worldwide began confronting the issues facing the church.

Four days before the pope would arrive, about 270 delegates, most in their 20s, convened the first formal activity of World Youth Day.

The International Youth Forum at Regis University, a small Jesuit college in north Denver, would groom its participants to become leaders of many World Youth Day conferences.

The delegates dressed in dashikis, kilts, sarongs, business suits and that most universal of uniforms — T-shirts and Levis.

They sat awestruck when Kathleen Friel, 19, a Houston college student, pulled herself to her feet and began speaking, struggling valiantly with her cerebral palsy to make herself understood.

"I think there is a reason why God gave me this," she said haltingly. "I view it as a kind of gift. Part of the reason why God gave me this is so I can try to make the church and society as a whole more open to people with disabilities."

Her listeners gave her thunderous applause.

As the momentous events began to unfold, the flocks of committed young visitors plunged into a week that would change their lives.

Pope John Paul II would soon be among them.

Celebration Plaza

For more than three hours, nearly unbroken lines of devout young Catholics streamed toward Celebration Plaza. Thousands of pairs of white sneakers moved in unison. As the afternoon heat ebbed and the sun began its descent over the Rocky Mountains, the sense of anticipation grew palpable.

World Youth Day had begun.

An estimated 100,000 people crowded fervently into the plaza to witness the official opening Mass.

The young people had come and gone all afternoon, sampling a musical cavalcade headlined by country-and-western star Wynonna Judd. Now they were back — to get closer to God.

The faithful wore baseball caps, straw sombreros and foam miters. Spanish kids from Valencia chanted and sang. Vietnamese waved riotously colored kites.

Celebration Plaza throbbed.

The graceful Greek architecture of the park, framed by Denver's angular skyline and the grand gold dome of the Colorado Capitol, made a handsome global amphitheater.

As the richly robed priests gathered on the huge altar, World Youth Day ambassadors shouted hello to the throng in seven languages, then asked delegations to sing out a greeting in their own tongue.

Aided by a phalanx of distinguished clergy, J. Francis Stafford, Denver's archbishop, led the worldwide assembly in Holy Communion.

"May your generation of Christians make a difference," he told his youthful congregation, then added this challenge:

"God is entrusting to the church in the 21st century the task of keeping the spirit of childhood alive in the world."

The sun had shone brightly, and now the clear, cool evening energized the young pilgrims. Tired but happy, they hiked back to their buses, hotels or open-air sleeping quarters.

It had been a day to get the feel of a great city, make friends and begin the serious business of worship and reflection.

Symbols of devotion, a cross and rosary propel Carmen Ramos of Puerto Rico in prayer during the opening Mass at Celebration Plaza.

GLENN ASAKAWA

THOMAS KELSEY

Framed by Denver's skyline and the gold-domed Colorado Capitol, Civic Center Park, renamed Celebration Plaza for the week, fills with worshipers (above) for the opening Mass. Proudly displaying their flag, French delegates (left) seize a perch with a commanding view. Buttons, souvenirs and other paraphernalia adorning a vendor's booth (top left) are testament to the popularity of this pope.

The shallow pool at Celebration Plaza (above left) beckons the weary and the over-heated beneath the blazing Colorado sun. Becky Alexander, 15, of Colorado (above right) shows just how good the water feels. A cool splash (left) takes the edge off the searing midday heat.

LINDA McCONNELL

GLENN ASAKAWA

*A procession of priests moves through Celebration Plaza (above) for the opening
Mass that attracted 100,000. To feed the multitudes during Holy Communion, tens
of thousands of wafers (left) must be readied for distribution. Bishops (top left) greet
the throngs of worshipers at the first official event of World Youth Day.*

STEVE GROER

*Country and western
star Wynonna Judd
(right) thrills thou-
sands as World Youth
Day begins with a noon-
time musical flourish.
In the shadow of a clas-
sic Colorado cowboy
(far right), young people
revel in Judd's stirring
performance.*

STEVE GROER

In the rugged foothills west of Denver, young pilgrims climb the 373 steps at the Mother Cabrini Shrine, paying homage to Colorado's only saint. Not many go straight to the top. They stop and pray along the way.

GLENN ASAKAWA

Feeling for a minute like sardines, Swiss delegates pack the Sixteenth Street Mall shuttle (top). The buses ferried delegates through downtown all week long. Chris Martin of Denver (center in picture at right) joins in the Celebration Plaza revelry with the youth ministry from Bend, Ore., during the Wynonna Judd concert. Angling for a better view, young people watch from a sculpture in Celebration Plaza (far right).

THURSDAY, AUGUST 12, 1993
The Pope's Arrival in Denver

The two airborne behemoths exuded power. As the 747s dropped from leaden skies and landed at Stapleton International Airport, they made Denver, for a brief time, the capital of the world.

The world's most influential religious leader was about to meet the leader of the world's most powerful country.

First, Air Force One taxied to a halt in front of the reviewing stand, and President Bill Clinton, joined by his wife Hillary and daughter Chelsea, stepped off to a warm welcome.

Slightly more than an hour later, Shepherd One, the sleek green, white and red Alitalia 747 carrying Pope John Paul II, cruised to a halt.

The president and the pope greeted each other with smiles and prolonged handshakes.

"John Paul Two, we love you," chanted several hundred spectators ecstatic to have been selected to welcome the pope.

"The United States is honored to have you in Denver," the president told the pope as a downpour began.

John Paul thanked the president and praised the American people. The spiritual leader of nearly 1 billion Roman Catholics also had an unmistakable message:

"If you want equal justice for all, and true freedom and lasting peace, then, America, defend life. All the great causes that are yours today will have meaning only to the extent that you guarantee the right to life."

Then the Holy Father joined the chief executive and pressed close to the people, grasping a sea of outstretched hands, smiling back at faces filled with reverence, kissing a baby with curly blond hair.

The Rocky Mountain West embraced Pope John Paul.

HAL STOELZLE

Pope John Paul II, framed in the doorway of Shepherd One (right), waves to the crowd at Stapleton International Airport upon arriving in Denver. American bishops show their delight in welcoming the Holy Father to Denver (above). President Clinton, first lady Hillary Rodham Clinton and daughter Chelsea join the happy procession.

JAY KOELZER

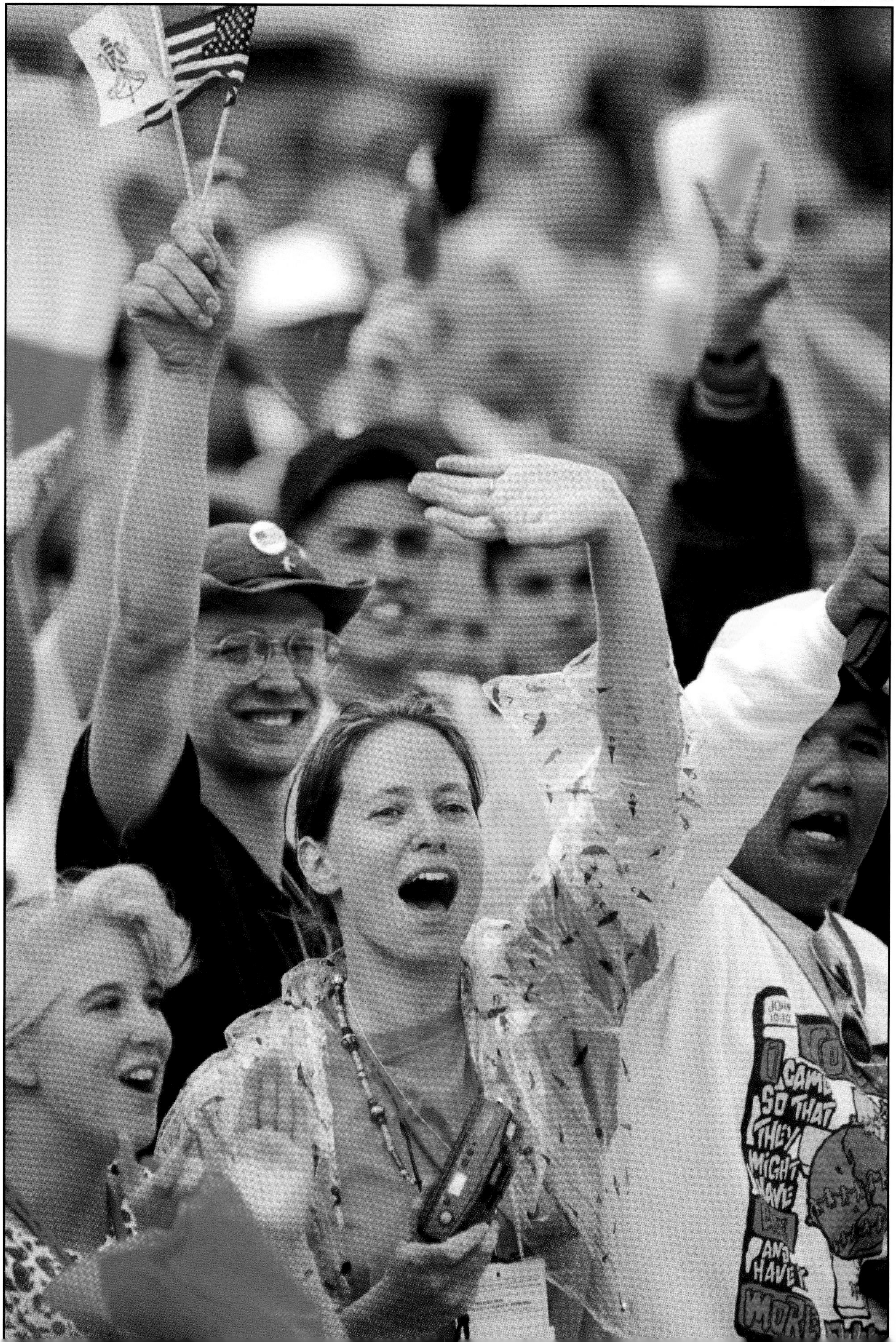

HAL STOELZLE

JAY KOELZER

Bedazzled by the presence of two major world leaders, young people cheer the pope and the president at the airport (left). Colorado community leaders welcome the Clintons to Denver (top). Two members of the traveling party aboard Shepherd One (above) take in the spectacle of the pope's arrival in Denver.

'I come to Denver to listen to the young people gathered here, to experience their inexhaustible quest for life.'

– Pope John Paul II

JAY KOELZER

Twin umbrellas shield the pope and president from a steady downpour during the arrival ceremony at Stapleton International Airport. It wasn't quite as good as an umbrella, perhaps, but a chair (left) keeps the rain off a spectator at the airport.

President Clinton leads the cheers for John Paul. "Your Holiness," the president begins, "the United States is honored to have you in Denver."

HAL STOELZLE

President Clinton and Pope John Paul II savor the enthusiasm of the crowd welcoming them at the airport.

'*If you want equal justice for all, and true freedom and lasting peace, then, America, defend life. All the great causes that are yours today will have meaning only to the extent that you guarantee the right to life.*'
– Pope John Paul II

Undeterred by a cascade of rain (above), the president and the pope converse after the airport arrival ceremony. The pope takes his seat (right) for the short helicopter hop to Regis University while President Clinton heads for his own aircraft.

THURSDAY, AUGUST 12, 1993

Regis University

After the adulatory outpouring at the airport, it was time for Pope John Paul II and President Clinton to meet privately. The place for their retreat was the tree-lined campus of Regis University in north Denver.

After they stepped off separate helicopters and greeted a select receiving line of well-wishers affiliated with the school, the two world leaders strode into the 106-year-old stone-and-brick center of the Jesuit university. They chatted animatedly while dozens of photographers recorded the scene.

When the cameras left and the doors closed, the pope and the president tackled some of the world's overriding problems. Bosnia. The Middle East. Somalia. Their conversation wasn't going to solve the hatred and deprivation that riddle the globe. But the private hour they spent together perhaps allowed each man to take measure of the other.

They exchanged gifts — the president giving the pope a walking stick with an angel carved on top, the pontiff giving Clinton a Bible.

Their meeting concluded, pope and president emerged into the daylight and ambled onto the campus' grassy, tree-lined commons to read brief statements. The president, joined by his wife and daughter, bid John Paul goodbye.

The Holy Father now was ready to mingle with the world's young people.

Regis University, a Jesuit center of learning in north Denver, played host to a discussion of world affairs between Pope John Paul II and President Clinton.

The pope and president stroll the commons at Regis University (left), where they conferred for an hour on world affairs. "I am pleased, Mr. President, that we have had this opportunity to talk together about some of the principal concerns of the world," the pope says. The pope and president (below) banter before beginning their world affairs discussion at Regis University.

THURSDAY, AUGUST 12, 1993
Mile High Stadium

F OR 90,000 enraptured Christians, the moment was at hand.

The centerfield scoreboard in Mile High Stadium flashed an exultant message: "Now is the time!"

Into this vast human sea rode Pope John Paul II. If fatigue from his long journey was tugging at him, he did not show it.

He radiated good cheer, excitement, compassion, hope and determination.

A chilly rain soaked the stadium as the pope made

his way inside, but it could not quell the joy in the hearts of the multitudes. A blessed few got to touch the pope — and be touched by him. He softly cradled the face of a reverent young woman, her delicate fingers brushing the sleeves of his cassock.

The unforgettable moments came almost without ceasing.

"This World Youth Day," Pope John Paul began, "has brought us to Denver, a stupendous setting in the heart of the United States of America."

Gazing out into the largest crowd ever to fill this

A forest of umbrellas sprouts (below left) as a downpour moves in before the pope's arrival at Mile High Stadium. The rain failed to discourage the faithful. Clergy (below right) were a prominent part of the huge gathering.

KEN PAPALEO

CYRUS McCRIMMON

venerable stadium, John Paul offered a burnished fragment of biblical eloquence from the Book of Revelation: "I greet each one of you: 'A great multitude which no man could number, from every nation, from all tribes and peoples and tongues.'"

Pat Matthews, 16, of Philadelphia, might have been speaking for just about everyone:

"We spent days on a bus to get here, traveled halfway across the country, all scrunched up together, and this makes up for it. This makes up for everything we've been through."

When it was time to close, the pope showed his humility.

"My speech was long, was too long," he said with a touch of sheepishness.

And then he gave the pilgrims reason to await the momentous events of the next three days.

"Dear young friends, in the name of Jesus Christ I greet you and bless you! With great joy I look forward to our next meeting.

"Hasta la vista!"

The pilgrims erupt into pandemonium (left) as the popemobile arrives with John Paul. Young Vietnamese-American Catholics (below) signal their joy.

Unbridled joy reigns in Mile High Stadium as the pope makes his entrance.

Carmelite nuns wave ecstatically, clutching the banner that symbolizes their devotion to God and the church.

ELLEN JASKOL

Feeling the power of the moment, Bobbie Jo Roman (above) of Odessa, Texas, joins hands with friends as Mile High Stadium rocks for the Holy Father. Exuberant young people give John Paul a boisterous Mile High welcome (above right). Tim Loucks of Grand Junction, Colorado, shares emotions with Sue Ryan of Minneapolis (right) as they listen to the pope in a wheelchair-accessible portion of the stadium.

GLENN ASAKAWA

DEAN KRAKEL

DEAN KRAKEL

"I greet each one of you: 'A great multitude which no man could number, from every nation, from all tribes and peoples and tongues.'"

John Paul blesses one of the many awestruck believers who had the privilege of meeting the Holy Father at Mile High Stadium. There is standing room only as 90,000 joyous Catholics (far right) deliver an uproarious welcome to the pope.

ELLEN JASKOL

KEN PAPALEO

In words befitting this most international of popes, the Mile High Stadium scoreboard (left) offers a welcome in six languages. Vietnamese-Americans from Chicago (below) cheer the pope at the stadium. On the pope's final day in Denver, Vietnamese-Americans enjoyed a festive audience with him.

ELLEN JASKOL

*As the sun sets behind the stadium, 90,000 spectators experi-
ence unrestrained joy with the spiritual leader of their faith.*

CYRUS McCRIMMON

FRIDAY, AUGUST 13, 1993
Tent City

Friday was the quiet day. Revelry turned to reflection.

The morning after the boisterous Mile High Stadium rendezvous between the pope and 90,000 exhilarated followers, John Paul celebrated Mass with 450 of his bishops at the gloriously renovated Cathedral of the Immaculate Conception. A Marine helicopter then carried him to one of the symbolic highlights of his trip to America: a day of rest and contemplation in the Rocky Mountains.

The wilderness surrounding the Catholic retreat at St. Malo might have reminded the pope of the Tatra Mountains of his native Poland. The columbines were blooming, and the firs, brooks and lush ground cover at 9,200 feet elevation were a welcome tonic for the Holy Father on the fifth day of a rigorous trip.

Back in Denver, World Youth Day's foot soldiers, now numbering a staggering 186,000, spent the day at Mass, catechism and workshops. Some repaid Denver for its hospitality by planting trees, building houses for the poor and cleaning up litter.

Thousands seeking inspiration visited Mother Cabrini Shrine, the hilltop monument to Colorado's only saint. The pilgrims climbed the 373 steps to a 22-foot statue of Christ, pausing along the way to catch their breath and murmur "Our Father" and "Hail Mary."

The day closed with the solemn Stations of the Cross ritual before 60,000 at Mile High Stadium.

When it was time for John Paul to leave the mountains and return to Denver, the world once again saw the remarkable bond this pope has with the people. He slowly walked several hundred yards down a country road to greet 150 well-wishers who had waited hours hoping to glimpse this most famous of visitors. He touched hands, foreheads and cheeks and thanked the astonished gathering.

One Denver television station carried the impromptu meeting live for 19 unforgettable minutes. Said the news director: "Everyone in the control room watched in amazement. No one said a word."

If pilgrims expect some deprivation along the way, Sara Gilbert, (left), and Steffanie Gomes, both 17, have surely found it. Their early-morning showering at Fitzsimons Army Medical Center's tent city calls for a little creativity.

BRIAN GADBERY

Joe Gauche (right in picture above), 15, entrusts his face to Mike McDonald, 16, for a morning shave at the Fitzsimons tent city. Gauche and McDonald, both of North Bend, Oregon, were among 520 delegates from the Pacific Northwest who were housed at Fitzsimons. In the communal living quarters, morning for Larry Weber of Aloha, Oregon, starts with a splash of cold water (right) from a big pot.

*Lena Smith, 20, of Portland, Oregon, receives the sacra-
ment of confession (left) at the tent city from Father
Edward Kucera, Catholic chaplain at Fitzsimons.
Early morning is a time for tent city residents (above) to
rouse and regroup.*

FRIDAY, AUGUST 13, 1993
Bishop's Mass

HAL STOELZLE

Framed by towering architecture and sculpture (above), the bishops' processional heads into the Cathedral of the Immaculate Conception for Mass with the pope. Showing strength in numbers, 450 bishops fill the cathedral (right) to hear the pope tell them to minister to young people.

FRIDAY, AUGUST 13, 1993

St. Malo Retreat

'This World Youth Day has brought us to Denver, a stupendous setting in the heart of the United States of America.'

– Pope John Paul II

VATICAN POOL PHOTOGRAPH

Alone with his thoughts (below), John Paul spends part of Friday reading in the splendor of the Rocky Mountains at the St. Malo retreat, elevation 9,200 feet. Sporting a new pair of athletic shoes (below left), the pope hikes through the woods at St. Malo.

FRIDAY, AUGUST 13, 1993
Stations of the Cross

Pilgrims relive the suffering of Jesus during the solemn Stations of the Cross ritual (far right) at Mile High Stadium. Some pilgrims are deeply moved (bottom right) during the service. Geraldo Gutierrez Golaviz of Los Angeles, absorbed in the evening's quiet, contemplative mood, cradles his guitar (near right) during the observance.

KEN PAPALEO

GLENN ASAKAWA

LINDA McCONNELL

SATURDAY, AUGUST 14, 1993
Mass for International Youth Forum Delegates

Pope John Paul II had come to America with a message. Today was his day to deliver it.

In an address to 18,000 Colorado Catholics at McNichols Arena, Pope John Paul set an uncompromising moral tone. He harshly condemned abortion, urban violence and sexual misconduct by the church's own priests.

The pope had begun the day with Mass for the young leaders of World Youth Day. Afterward, he took time to meet each of the 270 delegates to the International Youth Forum. They filed slowly past the altar, kneeling in front of him to receive a blessing and whisper their admiration.

For the pilgrims of World Youth Day, today was the day for The Trek — the 15-mile walk from downtown to Cherry Creek State Park. There, they came together for a night-long vigil preceding Sunday's papal Mass.

The pilgrimage captured the city's imagination. Well-wishers lined the route, waving from atop every overpass.

As dusk spread over a hushed crowd of 250,000 at Cherry Creek, the pope continued his attack on contemporary morality. He sternly rebuked "an anti-life mentality, an attitude of hostility to life in the womb and life in its last stages."

"Young people," he implored his young listeners, "do not give in to this widespread false morality. Do not stifle your conscience!"

The pope appeared deeply moved by the assemblage. During interludes of stirring music such as Barber's *Adagio for Strings*, John Paul tightly shut his eyes, his left hand pressing against his cheek.

The dignity and emotion of the prayer vigil soothed the pilgrims. Tears trickled down the cheeks of many.

The thousands who had completed the long, hot hike from downtown had suffered their share of blisters and exhaustion. Now, in the cool darkness, they settled in for the night, invigorated and inspired.

HAL STOELZLE

Swaying to the music, young people join hands (below) and share the spirit that brought them together at a Mass for the leaders of World Youth Day. The pope (below left) delivered a 30-minute homily at the Mass for International Youth Forum delegates, comparing them to the 12 apostles who spread Christ's teachings.

Frank Rocha, 25, of Amarillo, Texas, weeps as he embraces the pope after Mass. Mary Oswald of Mendham, New Jersey (below), was one of many disabled young people moved by the pope's Mass Saturday at the cathedral.

HAL STOELZLE

HAL STOELZLE

SATURDAY, AUGUST 14, 1993
Pilgrimage to Cherry Creek State Park

LINDA McCONNELL

Streaming out of downtown, pilgrims (right) begin the 15-mile hike to Cherry Creek State Park, headed for a night-time prayer vigil and Sunday's outdoor Mass. Sister Tracey Reed (above) of Paterson, New Jersey, strides toward the state park. She was one of tens of thousands of pilgrims who made the trek.

Weary pilgrims trudge into Cherry Creek State Park (right) at the end of a long, hot journey that left many blistered, dehydrated and otherwise exhausted. While the knapsacks seemed to weigh more the longer the pilgrims walked (above), an umbrella to block the relentless sunlight was worth its weight in gold.

SATURDAY, AUGUST 14, 1993

McNichols Arena

Pope John Paul II uses an audience with Colorado Catholics at McNichols Arena to confront some of the most difficult questions facing the church. Native American dancers (below right) celebrate their culture for the pope at McNichols. Love comes in all sizes (top right) at the meeting with Colorado Catholics.

CYRUS McCRIMMON

CYRUS McCRIMMON

CYRUS McCRIMMON

SATURDAY, AUGUST 14, 1993
Cherry Creek State Park Vigil

LINDA McCONNELL

An excited young woman stands above the crowd (right), anticipating the pope's arrival at Cherry Creek State Park for Saturday night's prayer vigil. Young people at the park might have been tired, but they still had plenty of steam to burn off before the vigil (above).

Clockwise from right: Crosses to commemorate World Youth Day were plentiful, thanks to vendors at the park before the prayer vigil. A cross serves as a staff of life for one pilgrim, who has lashed a sleeping bag and other vital possessions to this most Christian of symbols. A member of the Crow tribe gives a blessing during the Native American presentation before the vigil. Banners, flags and umbrellas add zest to the sea of humanity at Cherry Creek State Park.

DEAN KRAKEL

BRIAN GADBERY

GLENN ASAKAWA

An international assembly of flags (left) frames the pope and his bishops as he leads the vigil Saturday evening. Rapt in attention as Pope John Paul II speaks, young people keep their candles burning (right) to illuminate the night.

THOMAS KELSEY

DEAN KRAKEL

As darkness sets in, fervent pilgrims from St. Patrick's Church in St. Louis (above) show that their spirit has not waned. Stoic as wax melts on his hand, Tom Horton, 18, of Denver, spreads light during the prayer vigil (above right). His cousin, Amalia Solano, 15, of Quincy, Massachusetts, listens intently. Rudy Cosac, 24, of Guatemala (right), spends three hours in prayer at Saturday night's vigil.

ELLEN JASKOL

DEAN KRAKEL

GLENN ASAKAWA

SUNDAY, AUGUST 15, 1993
Papal Mass, Cherry Creek State Park

As dawn broke, a cobalt sky and brilliant sunshine enveloped Cherry Creek State Park. For the pilgrims of World Youth Day and thousands of Coloradans assembled with them, Mass with Pope John Paul II would be the event's spiritual pinnacle.

After a weeklong emotional and physical endurance test at mile-high altitude, the multitudes were ready for a sharply focused directive. The pope gave them one.

"At this stage of history," he told them, "the liberating message of the gospel of life has been put into your hands. And the mission of proclaiming it to the ends of the Earth is now passing to your generation."

The crowd numbered 375,000. Indeed, the sun took its toll — about 14,000 suffered from dehydration, exhaustion or other infirmities. But physical discomfort could not still the pilgrims' pride.

"We came together to pray," summed up Rene Pechura, 23, who lives near Frankfurt, Germany. "That's going to make a difference all over the world, now and well into the future."

From Cherry Creek, the pope returned to McNichols Arena for a rousing meeting with Vietnamese-American Catholics. Then, in one poignant, final stop, he visited the Mount St. Vincent Home for abused children.

The kids clustered around John Paul, peppering him with questions. Fighting off weariness, he joined hands with them in a circle as they sang a farewell.

"Thanks for making the pope very happy," he said.

As Shepherd One departed Stapleton to carry the pope back to Rome, a warm afterglow lingered over the city.

A worldwide congregation of young Roman Catholics had wrapped Denver in a long, loving embrace. The city's people seemed to draw strength and renewal from the waves of hope and good feeling that washed over them.

World Youth Day 1993 had been, quite simply, a triumph.

Dawn comes to Cherry Creek State Park. One by one, sleeping pilgrims awake and make ready for the papal Mass, the climax of World Youth Day.

THOMAS KELSEY

A panorama of pilgrims spread out before him, Pope John Paul II celebrates Holy Communion before 375,000 worshipers at Sunday's Mass.

Beneath a glorious Colorado blue sky (right), young people worship with the pope. John Paul offers a private prayer (above) during the Mass.

The pope blesses Native Americans (left) at the service. Worshipers receive Holy Communion (above) in the bright morning sunshine. Treasuring the moment, Brad Evans, 14, Tammy Fischer, 24, and Rachel Gaes, 13, linger after Sunday's Mass (top), ready to carry their faith home.

Eric Schaffhausen gives water to fellow Minnesotan Mary Oellerich to treat her exhaustion and dehydration (far right). More than 14,000 were stricken by the elements Sunday. Ignoring the heat, Brother Francis (below) of the Libertyville, Illinois, Franciscans, holds an intravenous bottle for Jan Ward, 15, of San Diego, after she was overcome by heat exhaustion. Young people battle dehydration and fatigue in the heat after the Mass (right).

DENNIS SCHROEDER

DAVID DENNEY

DENNIS SCHROEDER

Discomfort was commonplace during the day at Cherry Creek State Park. Long lines at portable toilets (left) were common. Workers (above) tried to keep the supply lines working.

Dan Pizarro, 15, (left in picture at right) and his brother Cesar, 17, of Englewood, Colorado, painted the pope's likeness on each other. Helping a friend look her best, Josefina Naranjo touches up Elvia Esquivel's lipstick (below) before the Mass. The two 13-year-olds from Washington state endured the summer heat to worship with the pope. Water from a provident fire hose cools the crowd at the hot, dusty Mass site (far right).

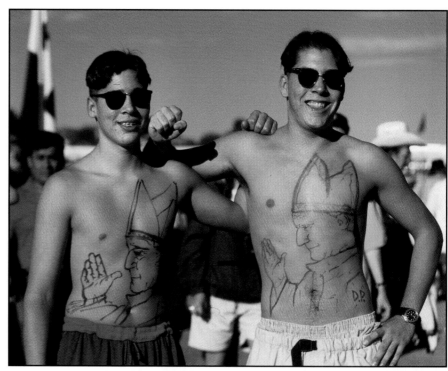

STEVE GROER

JAY KOELZER

SUNDAY, AUGUST 15, 1993
Vietnamese at McNichols Arena

Clockwise from top: Vivid Vietnamese costumes, music and other traditions highlight a special papal audience. The pope welcomes Vietnamese-American Catholics. A capacity crowd gives the pope a heartfelt reception. A contemplative Dzung Tong, 20, of Denver, watches Vietnamese-Americans celebrate their culture.

CYRUS McCRIMMON

CYRUS McCRIMMON

ount St. Vincent Home

DEAN KRAKEL

The final stop on Pope John Paul's itinerary, before depart-ing for the airport, is the Mount St. Vincent home for abused children. John Paul embraces the children (right), then joins hands with them (above) as they sang a farewell.

'He gives us courage. As we reflect together on the life which Jesus gives, I ask you to have the courage to commit yourselves to the truth. Young people of the world, hear his voice. Hear his voice and follow him!'

– Pope John Paul II